T.S. Davis Philosophy of Life Poems

T.S. Davis

ISBN: 9781984102942
ISBN 9781984102942-:

DEDICATION

To Him, Her, They and Them…

CONTENTS

1   1:23   1

2   2:22   Pg. # 9

3   3:33   Pg. # 16

4   4:02   Pg. # 20

5   4:13   Pg. # 28

6   12:12   Pg. # 34

7   7:12   Pg. # 37

8   9:10   Pg. # 52

9   9:17   Pg. # 75

10   11:11   Pg. # 83

THIS IS BOOK IS NOT FOR EVERYONE. IT IS FOR THOSE WHO NEED IT. THOSE WHO FEEL LIKE THEY HAVE NO VOICE SIMPLY BECAUSE THEY HAVE NOT DISCOVERED IT YET. THOSE WHO DON'T FEEL INTELLIGENT ENOUGH TO SPEAK OUT. THOSE WHO QUESTION THEIR DESIRE TO BE HEARD. THOSE WITH SOLUTIONS TO QUESTIONS THEY BELIEVE THEY ARE NOT ARTICULATE ENOUGH TO ANSWER. THIS BOOK IS FOR ANYONE WHO CAN RELATE OR BENEFIT FROM THE TRIALS, TRIBULATIONS, INTERNAL TURMOIL, FAITH, PURPOSE, PUSHING,OVERCOMING, PERSEVERANCE, AND THE LONG DAYS AND NIGHTS OF CRYING SILENT DRY TEARS THAT IT TOOK TO WRITE IT. IT IS FOR THOSE THAT NEED TO BE REMINDED THAT THOUGH THEY MAY BE COMPLETELY UNAWARE OF THEIR GOD GIVEN GIFTS , THERE ARE PEOPLE WITH THEIR EARS TO THE WIND YEARNING TO HEAR THEIR VOICE AND THEIR EYES TO THE SKY WAITING FOR THEM TO BECOME THE STARS THAT THEY WERE BORN TO BE.

REMEMBER YOUR PURPOSE IS NOT EXCLUSIVE TO YOU IT IS AN EXTENSION OF GOD MANIFESTED ON EARTH THROUGH YOU TO HELP SERVE HIS PEOPLE.

CHAPTER 1
1:23 AM

By Learning to make peace with the pieces of me that are unbecoming, based upon the world's expectations...

I am walking my purpose path toward true happiness.
T.S. Davis

Can We?

I mean
Can we really?
Do we ever truly?

Choose who we love???

Do we know the difference between?
Soulmate, obligation, and lust?

Is the person we love always the same person that we trust?

If they should be one in the same
Perhaps we've been giving the wrong person the wrong name...

Love should equal trust
Desire should equal lust
Obligation should equal must...

Only when all 3 is found in one can we say we made a choice

Some of you say we can choose
Without adhering to these rules
But I feel compelled to ask,

Can we...
T.S. Davis

You removed my writer's block and all of my inhibitions
All of my previous apprehensions no longer have any
restrictions.

Untitled thoughts...

You wanted to excite just enough love
To ignite jealousy
You being the cause of someone else's heart casualty
Didn't factor into the equation of your fantasy

You found someone full of empathy then cut, sliced and drained them
out on the brokenness of your fragility

Only by God's grace and Choosing humility
Does that someone gain the ability
To deal with the pain
Then find a way to regain
The motivation to love that you stripped away from their brain

Reminding themselves that giving love freely could never be done in
vain
And no matter what a peasant does
They must always do what royalty does
And Reign.

1:23 AM Untitled thoughts...

Our souls our are intertwined
I'm yours and you're mine
Since the beginning of time
This love was predestined and Divine
There is no mountain I wouldn't climb
There is no sea I wouldn't sail
There is no one I wouldn't tell
Our love is purposed to prevail.

Nothing or no one
Could ever cause it to fail
You are the cure and cause
To my butterflies
The twinkle in my eyes
My foreseeable surprise
Yeah I knew you were coming
I just didn't know when
You are the love of my life
That came disguised
As my friend
So happy that when
The time was right
We both gave in.

You Deserve...

You deserve the very best version of
Me
You deserve the me that is free from
Fear and insecurities

The me that tries to hit the high notes of songs knowing I can't sing

The me that tries to learn a new dance move no matter how ridiculous I think I may look

The me that is ready and willing to recite
My poetry in front of perfect strangers or my extra irritating family

The me that knows how to embrace life and enjoys the preciousness of its seconds while I'm experiencing them

I know that you're not looking for love while God is working on you

I understand completely because he is working on me too
I know

Because that is what,

You deserve...

How...

Does one define hurt?
By the aches in the unseen crevices of their souls

By the inability to control emotions that seem like they have a mind of
their own

Does one define brokenness
By the pieces of themselves, they can no longer find
Or...
By the pieces of their soul filled with anguish that they try
So desperately to hide

How does one get over all the intense pressures they've been under?

How...

You won't see me cry…

Though I'm shattered into pieces
You cannot see with the naked eye

You won't see me cry…
Though my heart goes un mended and love hurts to even try

You won't see me cry…

As I sit full of forgiveness giving God full repentance while I breathe deep and sigh

You will not see me cry…

As I sit in sheer disbelief, confused, betrayed and wondering why?

You will not see me cry…

Why?

If I left here today
And I could only see you
Through the veil
Knowing that I made sure
That you knew
I loved you
Is the only way I could rest
Peacefully at the end of our tale

So I say it often
I show you in all of the ways that I know how

You were the best costar to my life movie
So at the end take a bow

You displayed the best character
Though you were no character

You were completely authentic
Anytime you said anything
I knew without a doubt that you
Meant it

You brought me clarity in a world
Full of darkness and disparities

Your transparency
Transcended me pass the limits of my complacency

Allowing me to be
truly open Free and accepting of she
Who is I
I love you and I thank you for
Being my,
Why...9-23-18?

Enough...

Tired of trying to show my true colors
To those who only choose to see gray

Those who hear me but choose not to listen
To anything that I say

Pain has never felt good
It is simply an all too familiar feeling
due to me not being loved the way that I should

My heart is becoming harder than wood
Made of the strongest hickory

No longer able to laugh away the disappointments of treats that turn out to be
Trickery

Wondering why it's so hard for me
To receive the love, I give consistently

Hoping that the path to love won't always be so rough

Praying that someday I won't be a way for someone to just pass the time

I will be the one they want for all time
I will be more than,

Enough...

Be love

Don't just show love or receive love from others

Embody all that love is with every fiber of your being

That is the only way to truly live your best life

Dear Creative Souls...

Write what hurts you most.
Write the thoughts that consume you
The ones you can't escape

Paint the images you feel in your soul and only see with pains internal eyes
Those are the portraits that may help another hurting soul survive

Sing the lyrics that cause trembles and teary eyes when people hear them
Sing the words that will help humanity
Break free from the demons within them

Rap the words you are afraid to say but know that you should
Rap your unique form of genius like no one else would
That is how you will change the world for good

Sculpt exactly what you see in your mind don't try to duplicate what the world has liked and seen in previous times

Bring forth to the world your gifts in the present
You are special because you're different
Not a copy of something that has already happened

Be you, Be authentic, Be Bold
That is the only way to truly Be Happy and Be free
My,

Dear Creative Souls...

The Writer's Creed...

Never interrupt the flow
Life will continue but you must never leave
Words trapped within you

When you feel the urge to write grab the nearest utensil

Pen, marker, pencil
Cellphone, laptop or tablet

Whichever is closest grab it

Free all of your creativity
release all your forbidden thoughts once held in captivity

Once stifled by the world's perceptions of masculinity and femininity

Women are more than sensitivity
And men are more than strength

People can be more than small minded
So write without fright and change the length of people's expectations

Don't just sit around complaining when you could be writing the words
that will change nations

You have the ability to do something that hasn't been done before you

You have the potential to exceed your own dreams

If you have to write until your fingers bleed to initiate change in
humanity

Write until red is all you see
That is the responsibility of those gifted into

The writer's creed...

**Don't hold me down
Lift me up.**

**Tell me why I should hold on
When I feel like giving up.**
T.S. Davis

??...
The question is not am I worthy to be loved...

The question is are you worthy of my love?

CHAPTER 3 3:33 AM

3:33 AM
I open my eyes
My thoughts drift directly to you

As if sleeping isn't the activity I would much rather do

One day a while ago
You held me close

Now the touch of your passion
Is what I desire most

I've been held, I've been kissed
But no one before you or since
Has made me feel like this

Your name echoes in my mind
Your touch causes me to tremble

Thoughts of your smile consume most of my time
Pure pleasure is exactly what you resemble

Perhaps one year, one day , one time
You won't just be a thought

But, You will be mine
At,

3:33 AM...

You Are My Thought's

3 am when I sit in my bed and words begin to flow like water into a tub with no drain

6 am when I'm standing in the shower pretending that each drop that hits my skin is the first may rain

9 am during my first class while trying to focus on psychology, visions of your smile keep reminding me why I love you

12 pm when I'm sitting and trying to eat my veggie pita. Wondering have you eaten yet

3 pm when I'm the first one in philosophy sitting and thinking about how my philosophy of life revolves around you

5 pm while in the kitchen cooking dinner wishing that I was cooking for you. Wishing all of your favorites dishes was something I knew.

8 pm in the shower envisioning myself washing your back while anticipating you slowly turning me to wash mine

9 pm while praying all of my thoughts will become reality. Praying that you're somewhere being prepared for me

10 pm when you are the leading man in all of my dreams...

12 am when my dreams become nightmares and I can feel the emotions that stem from every dream sequence or pain

3 am, when I sit up in my bed and words, begin to flow like water in a bathtub with no drain
It's because of you

You are,
My muse...
You Inspire me, consume all of me, you are officially,

My thoughts...

Last Day!

Feeling
Incompetent

From this moment on
Any goal I set I will accomplish it.

Today I have felt that I am less than I am
For the,

Last Day!

Silent Dry Tears...

Standing in the grocery store
Trying to budget the assistance
THEY think she shouldn't have
Mindful not to grab a bag of chips or cookies, for fear of condemnation

She cries
Silent, Dry Tears...

At the parent-teacher conference when
THEY ask "will Dad be joining us"?
She knows to say "not this time"
When the reality is "he might not ever"

She cries
Silent, Dry Tears

When she is cheering in the stands after bringing snacks, paying for sports uniforms, dance recital outfits, and all the dues, while in the back of her mind knowing she will be late on the bills that are due

She cries
Silent, Dry Tears

When her kids blame her for everything that goes wrong while reminding herself that **THEY** just don't know that is because of her and God that anything goes right

She Cries
Silent, Dry Tears

When she sits in class, trying to pass. Attempting to pay attention operating off 2 hours of sleep knowing **THEY** wouldn't understand if she broke down and began to weep.

She cries
Silent, Dry Tears

As she carefully types this poem mindful to explain only the tip of her struggle, never revealing the iceberg. Speaking for the single mothers whose voices go unheard, knowing that **THEY** can relate to each and every word...
She cries, Silent, Dry Tears...

CHAPTER 4 4:02 AM

Tired.

I'm tired of smiling when my face
Doesn't have the energy to move

I'm tired of pretending to care
When deep down I feel like I have nothing to prove

I'm tired of being everyone's shoulder to cry on,
Then when it's my turn there's nowhere for me to rest my eyes on

I'm tired of acting like I'm not tired

Tired of striving to be perfect, while constantly wondering is it even worth it

Tired of pretending to know my value, when most of the time I feel worthless

I could go on and on and on...
But I'm,

Tired.

I decided to live...

Today I took a deep breath of gratitude
And exhaled disappointment

I took a moment to appreciate the scent of life
I slowly breathed in optimism and hope
Exhaling pessimism and despair

I opened my eyes and decided to look at the world and see its beauty

I looked at the various shades of the sky
I looked at the ground covered by snow in the spring

I stood silent and listened to the birds sing
I heard the laughter of children as they were playing

In case you're wondering what is the point of what I'm saying...

The point is
That on today
I decided to live...

Today I am going to order a pizza
And enjoy every slice...
Because one day
I will be in shape
I will be wealthy
I will have all of my prayers answered
On that day
I will laugh about all the days I was worried
over nothing
Because on that day
I will realize that everything
Worked out exactly the way it was suppose
too...

My love when you find the one, may you feel like you can Fly
Hold hands, Jump, and Soar together!

MY HEART.

Sincerity, Clarity
Both rarities
That you embody so well
You radiate
Truth, Endurance, and perseverance
You are,

MY HEART.

Joy.

You will never be happy if your happiness Is dependent upon someone else because the moment they leave; your happiness will leave with them. You must find happiness within yourself only then will you begin to experience true everlasting,

Joy.

Once upon a time water was in love with fire because of how the heat made it feel. Whenever fire got close to water, the water felt warmth and passion, but whenever water tried to embrace fire, water would extinguish its flame ... Sometimes no matter how much you love someone you have to accept when your presence does more harm than good. You have the love them enough to walk away...

Chosen
God formed me straight from the mud…

CHAPTER 5 4:13 AM

Lessons

You learn more daily when you chose to pay attention

You grow from the storms that drench you and make you feel as though all is washed away

You emerge renewed just as the sun does after each dark damp night

You walk out renewed and refreshed filled with a brand new light

You make choices based on the wisdom of wrong vs right

You understand the difference between assumptions and understandings

You are better able to appreciate life once you learn to appreciate it's,

Lessons...

Distracted ...

I'm sorry I didn't watch you dance

I'm sorry that I didn't see you cry

Because this thing in my hands

Put me into a trance

I let social media

Distract me from being the most important thing that I am

A parent...

T.S. Davis

Know this...

When someone truly loves you it will not be a mystery to you or the world. You won't have to ask or wonder. They will state their intentions and do what is required to achieve them.
Until that moment comes and every moment after love yourself, cater to yourself and always remain mindful of what you deserve.

Promises to never break...

I promise to love, cherish and respect me

I promise to honor, encourage and never to neglect me

I promise to do for myself the way I do for others

I promise to remind myself of how special, unique and one of a kind a truly am

I promise to be the best version of me possible and to never take me for granted

I promise to thank God daily for creating me, myself and I.

Forever my muse...

Your positivity always gets to me
You speak with the heart of a poet

Your intellect is unmatched
You are the wise beyond your years I just wonder if you know it

Your optimism is astounding
You are the cause of my smiles and my happy tears

Your strength constantly strengthens me
You are the cure to my fears

Your creativity inspires me
You are the reason my heart speaks poetry it hasn't spoken in years

Your love is something I pray I never lose
You are my heart, my soul,

My Muse...

CHAPTER 6   12:12 AM/PM

Untitled Wisdom...

There will be times when you will not have time to think of the most
eloquent way to say something. At that moment don't waste time
trying to find words that you think will be acceptable. Just Say
something! Say what needs to be said! Say what others are afraid to
say.
Be Loud, Be Heard, Be You!

At that moment, at that time speaking the truth in the way that only
you can, is the most eloquent thing one can do.

There is something about walking in purpose
That completely destroys anything that attempts to
make you feel worthless...
T.S. Davis

When the time comes...

When someone puts you on a
Pedestal...
Don't step down
You may be the only person they find
admirable
You may be the only one capable
With providing them with hope for
humanity.

CHAPTER 7   7:12

In Life

I'm learning to stop being there
for others so much that I don't have enough of me here to help myself.

In life
T.S. Davis

You are

Such a unique puzzle
With thousands of scattered pieces
I get excited each time I discover a new segment of what makes you
You

I am witnessing an exquisite image being put together right before my eyes

You are simply magnificent
In my site

You are a masterpiece broken by those who were too foolish to comprehend your value

You are stronger than you know
Because you only acknowledge the parts of you that are fragile

You require special care and appreciation for the form of art that you are

You are an exceptional example of the beauty in humanities complexities

You are the physical representation of my soulmate manifested into reality,

You are...

Dear God

I lay on my face
With my arms stretched
You are the reason
All of needs have been met

I praise you for what is to come
Though it hasn't happened yet
For when you tell me it is so
Lord I trust you because
I know
That if you say stay, I should stay
But wherever send me I should
Go
You trust me with your Glow
May your light shine through me
You are the door to heaven
And my faith is the KEY

So I lay on my face
With my arms stretched
For you are the reason
I haven't gave up yet

Your Grace is sufficient,
Your love sustains me.
When the enemy
Thought he won
you
Showed up to claim me...

T.S. Davis

INFJ DOOR SLAM!

I am an INFJ
When you lie to me, you are not protecting
Me feelings
You are disrespecting my intuition and My
Intelligence

Once you have done this, please prepare for,
The Door Slam.

Control.

I've never been so happy
To not be in
Control
To ask permission
Before I make important
Decisions
To give up
Control
Without feeling controlled
To watch with sincere joy
As your plan for my life
Unfolds
God I thank you for guiding my steps
I thank you for loving me and making your presence in my life known
I thank you for being you
I thank you for willingness
to be in,

Control.

Thanks to you...

I write
And recite
Poems filled with insight
Into the depths of my soul

Thanks to you
I see and believe
I have the ability to become
Whom God has predestined me to be and I no longer stress about growing old

Thanks to you
I appreciate transforming daily into
The women I was born to be

Thanks to you I know you and now I know me

Thanks to you I am happier
Than I ever dreamed
I would be,

Thanks to you...

Choices

I asked myself why do I keep choosing darkness over light...
Maybe it's because in order to see darkness there must be a speck of light...
What I keep choosing is Hope...

I love
People love differently
Some people like minimal affection.
They don't like holding hands, cuddling, hugging, kissing or any other meaningful displays of affection.

Some people don't like texting, messaging or checking on one another out of sheer concern or just the desire to hear the other person voice...

All of the above is okay. The above statements are cool for other people, BUT...

For Me,
NEVER!
I love maximum affection
I want to hold hands and feel the warmth of my lover's fingers interlocked with mine.
I want to cuddle pressing every curve of my body against theirs.
I want to hug my love in just the right way so that I can hear the rhythm of his heartbeat.
I want to kiss him in a way that makes him forget any and everything other than my lips and our tongues exist at that moment.
I want to engage in every meaningful display of affection he or I can imagine.

I want to text and message my love then receive the same from him.
Checking on one another out of sheer concern or just to appreciate the sound of life, happiness, and pure excitement we help add to one another's voice..

The way I love does not come from a place of insecurity but the security that I feel knowing I'm giving all of my love to the right one.
The only one that,
I love...

Words to remember…

Being a leader is not about making a name
for yourself.
It is about the positive impact you make in
the lives of others
regardless of them knowing your name or
not.

T.S. Davis

COURAGE IS NOT THE ABSENCE OF FEAR IT IS
THE PRESENCE OF DETERMINATION.
T.S. DAVIS

BEING GRATEFUL IS MORE THAN BEING HAPPY
WHEN YOU GET EXACTLY WHAT YOU WANT. IT
IS BEING AWARE AND APPRECIATING THE
TIMES WHEN YOU GET WHAT YOU NEED, EVEN
WHEN IT IS NOT WHAT YOU WANT.

T.S. DAVIS

I Write...

These poems
I write daily
Attempting to fully display me

The hidden places of my being
That is usually
Unknown even to myself

The parts that I know must be revealed in order to ever truly connect to
someone else

The parts that hold but can't destroy the pain that I've felt

I write these poems with the hope that you will read them
And discover a way to find you

I write daily without fail
If I don't I will constantly
Yell at the tops of my lungs

I write so that when I die
I will be empty

Having written all the words to the songs I wish I could've sung
Knowing that singing was not my gift

Yet fulfilled knowing that
My gift is this
The pen and paper
That is my legacy and proof that
I did exist

Filled with my feelings, my process for healing, the proof of the power of
revealing the ugly honesty required to truly experience living
These are only a few of the vitally essential reasons,

I Write...

Only I can Write
I don't know how to write in abbreviations
I have too many passions

My words are like my breathing
Both intentional and unintentional actions

I write to my own satisfaction
But I do hope you like it

I write my Heart ,
My love ,
My life ,

Like,

Only I can write it...

As I sit in stillness.

Thinking about how
The night is silent calm and peaceful
It reminds me of myself
Mysterious and Intriguing
leaving many
Curious as to what they will find
If they attempt to explore me more
Dark, but also a bearer
Of some of the most beautiful light
To see into me clearly
One must have exceptional sight
Some see me and get excited
While others experience a sense of fright
Wondering if they should pursue
falling into deep contemplation about
what they should do
The funny thing is
I feel the unrest of uncertainty too,

As I sit in stillness.

CHAPTER 8   9:10

Distance...
The space between us
Even when side by side
Is too wide

Yet we must breath

Why does your air make me feel more alive?

In your presence I ask myself is this earth
or
Some unknown universe
my mere human mind
Lacks the words to describe

Our souls two asteroids predestined to collide

Transcending all space and time

As we became one in an instant our spirits intertwined

I feel you now
In every nerve of my spine

Every intricate impulse
The blood in my veins

My pleasure and my pain

I feel you in me
As if you are with me
Always
So in reality
what is,
Distance...

Why...?

Do I stare when you are simply being you?

I see you
I see beneath the layers of life's necessary cloak

I hear you
I hear the words that you haven't even spoke

I feel you
I feel you in ways your emotions haven't allowed you to know

I touch you
I touch you in my soul, so my hands know exactly where to go

I want you
I want you to reveal your truths that you never ever show

I desire you
I desire to be a part of the light that makes you glow

I crave you
I crave you in every way imaginable

I know you
I know that you are and will forever be my,

Why...?
By T.S. Davis

In your presence...

I feel safe
I feel secure
I feel sane

In your Presence

I know love
I know laughter
I know life

In your Presence

I have peace
I have purpose
I have passion

In your Presence

I am me
I am myself
I am more

In your Presence...

You Know...

You put your arm around my shoulder

You spoke only a few words

Though I saw your mouth move
Your soul is what I heard

You talked with me all night and we greeted the new day
With sleepy eyes and authentic smiles

You held me by the water and whispered in my ear
I felt so safe in your presence
I nearly forgot that falling in to the river is one of my biggest fears

You read my poems
I hid my tears

I watched you love, sacrifice and care for others
I knew that I loved you in a way that I could never love another

You affect me in so many incomprehensible ways

You wonder why I love you
so much but there are too many
Unexplainable reasons to name

I may not know what the future holds
But today
the only name written in my heart is...

You Know...

But...
You're rude
You seem so cold
You pull away

But
You're intriguing
You seem so warm
You pull me close

But
You're distant
You seem so uninterested
You pull my heart apart

But
You're here
You seem so in tuned
You pull my heart close to yours

But....

Life Moment...

I'm learning to fall in love slowly so that the impact of not being caught won't hurt so badly. Until the day I fall into the arms of my one true love and I never have to worry about hitting the ground ever again...

An unhealthy relationship is not one with which you experience loves conflict.

An unhealthy relationship is the internal conflict between your mind and heart that tortures your soul as you pretend you don't want to be with the person with which you have experienced loves conflict.

T.S. Davis

NEW
   DEEP THOUGHTS
   LONG NIGHTS
   IM WRONG YOU'RE RIGHT
   SMALL FIGHTS
   I WIN YOU LOSE
   TOO MANY POINTLESS POINTS
   TO PROVE
   OVERLY EMOTIONAL AND CONFUSED
   THOUGHTS LEFT UNSAID
   SAD THOUGHTS LEFT
   OCCUPYING OUR HEADS
   HEART TO HEARTS NEEDED
   WHEN WERE BOTH HEATED
   FOR REASONS THAT DEFY
   REASON
   TO BETRAY YOU WOULD BE
   THE ULTIMATE TREASON
   EVEN
   WHEN IT HURTS TO STAY
   NOTHING COULD JUSTIFY
   LEAVING
   THE DEFINITION OF MINE
   YOUR EYES TRANSLATES THE MEANING
   THROUGH EACH ONE
   I HEAR YOUR SOUL SPEAKING
   WHEN I CLOSE MINE
   YOU'RE THE STAR OF THE MOVIE THAT PLAYS WHILE IM SLEEPING
   YOU'RE MY CALMING CHAOS
   MY SOULS COMPASS
   WHEN I FEEL LOST
   YOU GUIDE ME
   BACK TO A PLACE OF REALITY
   MIXED WITH MY ULTIMATE FANTASY
   YOU BRING ME BACK TO YOU
   KNOWING THERE IS NO PLACE
   ID RATHER BE AND
   THERE IS ABSOLUTELY NOTHING
   THAT I'D RATHER DO
   EVEN AS WE AGE AND GROW GREY
   I KNOW THAT EACH DAY
   THAT I GROW WITH YOU
   WE WILL STILL FEEL THE CHEMISTRY
   AND BUTTERFLIES
   WE FELT WHEN OUR STORY BEGAN
   AND EVERYTHING WAS BRAND,
   NEW...

NEVER...

BEFORE OUR TONGUES
MADE LOVE TO THE RHYTHM
OF OUR PULSE

POTENTIALLY ...
BEFORE I BECAME WILLING
TO CHOOSE YOU, OVER ANYTHING
AT ANY COST

PERCHANCE...
BEFORE I LOOK INTO YOUR EYES
AND SAW I GLIMPSE
OF A PERFECT SOUL

POSSIBLY...
BEFORE GOD SHOWED
ME THE TWO OF US
STILL IN LOVE, WRINKLED, GREY AND OLD

PERHAPS...
BEFORE
MY THOUGHT'S BECAME CONSUMED
WITH GOD, PURPOSE, AND YOU

MAYBE, JUST, MAYBE
IN SOME OTHER LIFE, IN SOME OTHER DIMENSION
OR REALITY...
WE COULD HAVE BEEN BEST FRIENDS
BUT IN THIS ONE
IN THIS LIFE,
NEVER...

LOVE...

WHEN I THINK OF YOU
I CAN LET MY FEET HANG OFF THE BED
I CAN WRITE WITH MY BACK TOWARDS THE CLOSET
DOOR
I NO LONGER GET TENSE WHEN I HEAR CREEPY
CREAKING SOUNDS MADE BY MY OLD WOOD FLOOR

I DONT FEEL LIKE A BIRD WITH BROKEN WINGS

WITH YOU
I FEEL LIKE I SOAR
THROUGH THE INEVITABLE DIFFICULTIES OF LIFE

WHEN I THINK OF YOU IT FEELS LIKE THIS IT WHAT IT
FEELS LIKE
WHEN SOMEONE GETS IT RIGHT

WHEN I THINK OF YOU DEATH BECOMES BEAUTIFUL
ITS SIMPLY THE PERIOD
AT THE END OF A WELL LIVED LIFE

WHEN I THINK OF YOU AND ALL THAT YOUR LOVE
HAS EMPOWERED ME TO DO
I PRAY THAT MY PRESENCE IN YOUR LIFE HAS
ALLOWED YOU TO EXPERIENCE REAL, UNFILTERED,
LIFE TRANSFORMING,

LOVE...

I want...

TO LOOK IN YOUR EYES WHILE HOLDING YOUR
CHEEKS IN THE PALMS OF MY HANDS
WHILE FALLING MORE IN LOVE KNOWING THAT I'M
APART OF YOUR PLANS.

I WANT
TO FEEL YOUR LIFE ESSENCE ON MY CHEEKS
AS YOU TRY TO BREATH SOFTLY WHILE WATCHING
ME SLEEP

I WANT
TO KNOW WITH OUT ANY DOUBTS, WORRIES OR
ASSUMPTIONS, THAT I AM THE LOVE OF YOUR LIFE
AND YOU ARE MINE

I WANT
TO BELIEVE THAT OUR LOVE COMBINED WILL HEAL
ALL OF THE PAIN WE'VE ACCUMULATED OVER TIME

I WANT
TO BE WITH YOU NOW, AND FOR ETERNITY
EVEN WHEN MY SPIRIT IS ALL THAT'S LEFT OF ME,
YOU WILL FOREVER BE
ALL,

I WANT...

UNTIL YOU...

DIDN'T KNOW THOUGHTS FELT PAIN
AND EMOTIONS HAD THOUGHTS,

UNTIL YOU...

AM I...

THE ONE WHO MAKES YOU LOOK
OFF INTO THE DISTANCE
LOSING ALL FOCUS AND CONCENTRATION

THE ONE WHO MAKES YOU JUST A LITTLE NERVOUS YET
COMPLETELY COMFORTABLE BEING EXACTLY WHO YOU
ARE

THE ONE YOU ARE TERRIFIED TO LOSE
MAKING YOU FEEL LIKE YOU HAVE NOTHING, YET AT THE
SAME TIME EVERYTHING TO PROVE

THE ONE YOU KNOW WITHOUT DOUBT YOU MEAN THE
MOST TO BECAUSE I MEAN THE MOST TO YOU

THE ONE WHO'S PRESENCE MAKES YOUR HEART BEAT
FASTER
AND BRINGS A SMILE TO YOUR FACE WHEN REMINISCING
ON THE SOUND OF MY LAUGHTER

THE ONE THAT MAKES YOU REALIZE WHY GOD SAID ITS
NOT GOOD FOR MAN TO BE ALONE

THE ONE YOU KNOW THAT BESIDE YOU AND ONLY YOU IS
WHERE I BELONG

AM I THE ONE
WELL...

AM I...

AFRAID...

I'M TERRIFIED TO SAY THE WRONG THING
I NEVER WANT TO UPSET YOU.

I NEVER WANT TO BE THE CAUSE OF YOUR DARK
NIGHTS OF SECLUSION

I NEVER WANT TO BE THE REASON YOUR HEAD IS
SPINNING FULL OF CONFUSION

I WANT TO BE YOUR COMFORTING THOUGHTS
THE NAME THAT COMES TO MIND WHEN YOU NEED TO
CALM YOUR SOUL'S STORM

I WANT TO BE THE ONE THAT ALTERS THE
TEMPERATURE OF YOUR HEART AFTER YOU FACE THIS
COLD WORLD
KEEPING YOU WARM AND FILLED WITH PASSIONATE
FIRE

I WANT TO BE THE ONE WHO EMBODIES EVERY ONE
OF YOUR KNOWN AND SECRET DESIRES

BEING ANYTHING ELSE THAN THE ONE YOU WILL
LOVE FOREVER IS THE ONLY THING IN THIS WORLD
THAT MAKES ME,

AFRAID...

COULD YOU

LOVE MY UGLY
COULD YOU LOVE ME PAST
MY INSECURITIES AND THE THINGS SCRIPTURE
IDENTIFIES AS IMPURITIES

CAN YOU SEE PAST MY AESTHETICALLY PLEASING
PHYSICALITY

WOULD YOU RUN AWAY IF I REVEALED
THE THOUGHTS THAT FRIGHTEN ME
THE ONES THAT HAUNT ME AND MAKE ME TREMBLE

OR WOULD YOU HOLD ME
WHISPERING IN MY EAR AND REASSURING ME

THAT THOUGH LIFE IS TRULY FULL OF HORRIFYINGLY
PERPLEXING COMPLEXITIES

TRUE LOVE MAKES IT SIMPLE

LOOKING PASS MY PAST
ACCEPTING MY PRESENT
FULLY WELCOMING OUR FUTURE

IN THE WAY THAT ONLY
MY ONLY WOULD DO

THESE ARE QUESTIONS I CAN'T ANSWER, SO TELL
ME,

COULD YOU...

CHILDISH

LIKE I'M 16 BLUSHING
RUSHING TO SEE IF ITS YOU CALLING ME
EACH TIME MY PHONE RINGS

SCREAMING INTO MY PILLOW WHENEVER ITS SOMEONE ELSE
BECAUSE NO MATTER HOW HARD I TRY TO IGNORE THESE
FEELINGS I DONT WANT ANYONE ELSE

CHILDISH
LIKE I'M 16 PLANNING TO GO TO THE PROM ENVISIONING
MYSELF ON YOUR ARM AND DANCING THE NIGHT AWAY

FEELING SELFISH NOT WANTING TO SHARE YOU WITH
ANYONE ELSE

CRYING WHEN I DONT GET YOUR ATTENTION
STARING AT THE CEILING WISHING
YOU WERE CONSUMED WITH MUTUAL FEELINGS

CHILDISH
LIKE IM FULLY PREPARED TO HAVE A MENTAL TANTRUM WHEN
YOU DON'T DO THE THINGS I'VE
ENVISIONED IN MY MIND

FEELING LIKE THE DAYS DON'T HAVE ENOUGH TIME AND
TIME DOESN'T HAVE ENOUGH RESPECT

TO SLOW DOWN WHEN WE'RE IN EACH OTHERS
EMBRACE
GIVING YOUR HEART TIME TO REACT AND YOUR MIND
ENOUGH MOMENTS TO PROCESSS THE FACT
THAT YOU ARE THE ONLY ONE THAT CAN
MAKE ME ACT,

CHILDISH

I HONESTLY LOVE YOU...

LET ME HELP YOU HEAL
HIDING FROM ME IS PREVENTING THE FULFILLMENT OF MY
DESTINY.

I LOVE YOU IN WAYS WORDS WILL NEVER POSSESS
THE MAGIC TO EXPLAIN

I FELT YOU BEFORE I SAW YOU
THEN YOU APPROACHED ME

MY EYES COULD NOT CONTAIN THE REALITY OF YOU
SO I LOOKED AWAY

NOW EVERY MOMENT SINCE THAT DAY
OUR FIRST ENCOUNTER IS ON CONSTANT, CONSISTENT AND
CONTINUOUS REPLAY

I COULDN'T STOP IT IF I TRIED ITS ETCHED INTO MY PSYCHE

I DON'T KNOW HOW THIS HAPPENED BUT I KNOW THAT IT IS
MEANT

PREDESTINED AND PURPOSED
WE'RE SO CONNECTED MY HEART ACHES EACH TIME SOMEONE
MAKES YOU FEEL WORTHLESS

I CHOOSE TO WAIT FOR THE DAY I CAN GIVE YOU MY HEART
BECAUSE I KNOW YOU DESERVE IT

GIVING ME YOURS IN RETURN BECAUSE YOU KNOWT THAT I
WONT HURT IT

I KNOW I AM HERE TO UPLIFT, HONOR AND CHERISH YOU
I KNOW BEYOND ANY DOUBTS THAT,

I HONESTLY LOVE YOU..
.

MY...

YOU ARE SUCH A DREAM
YOU'RE MY EARLY MORNING THOUGHTS BEFORE I REALIZE
THAT I'M AWAKE

YOU'RE THE SUBSTANCE OF MY LIFE
MORE IMPORTANT THAN EACH BREATH THAT I TAKE

YOU'RE THE REASON I SEE MYSELF WALKING DOWN THE
AISLE IN WHITE SATIN AND EMBROIDERED LACE

THE MOST REMARKABLE IMAGERY MY EYES HAVE EVER
WITNESSED ARE ALL INTRICATELY PLACED IN VARIOUS
PARTS OF YOUR FACE

YOUR EYES ARE DEEP POOLS OF HAPPY SEDUCTION

YOUR NOSE OFTEN COLD TOUCHES MY CHEEKS AND I CANT
STOP BLUSHING

YOUR SMILE MY GOD YOUR SMILE CAN CAUSE VOLCANIC
IRRUPTIONS, PUT AN END TO CORRUPTION
AND SET CAPTIVES FREE

IT WOULD TAKE TWO ETERNITIES TO EXPLAIN THE EFFECTS
YOU HAVE ON EACH OF MY EXTREMITIES

I FEEL YOUR PRESENCE WITHIN EVERY INCH OF ME
EVEN WHEN YOU'RE MILES AWAY FROM ME

WHEN I AM WIDE AWAKE OR DEEP ASLEEP
YOU ARE,

MY...

T.S. Davis

TOUCH ME...

WITH NO HANDS
YOU PENETRATE EVERY FIBER OF MY BEING
EYES CLOSED FAST ASLEEP BUT I'M SEEING THE
POSSIBILITIES

ENVISIONING YOU IN MY PRESENCE
I CAN SMELL YOUR ESSENCE
YOUR SIGNATURE SCENT

I FEEL YOU
IT'S ASTOUNDING HOW YOU MAKE ME TREMBLE
FROM MILES AWAY

SIMPLY THINKING ABOUT YOUR EMBRACE PICTURING
YOUR HANDS AROUND MY WAIST
CAUSES TEARS TO STREAM SLOWLY DOWN MY FACE

HEART BEATING UNCONTROLLABLY
AT THE THOUGHT OF YOU HOLDING ME
YOUR VOICE GIVES YOU CONTROL OF ME

I'M ALMOST AFRAID TO SEE
HOW MY BODY WILL REACT WHEN YOU
ACTUALLY,

TOUCH ME..

70

MY LOVE,

YOUR SMILE IS LIKE THE GREATEST SIGHT
I'VE EVER SEEN

YOUR EYES ARE LIKE PURE LOVE AND MORE
INTRIGUING THAN ALL OF LIFE'S MOST PRECIOUS
THINGS

YOUR VOICE IS LIKE A CANDLES LIGHT
POWERFUL ENOUGH TO GUIDE ME, PEACEFUL AND
SERENE

YOU ARE MY CALM AND EXCITEMENT
MY SADNESS AND MY JOY

YOU HAVE THE ABILITY TO HURT ME OR HEAL ME
WITH A FLUCTUATION IN THE TONE OF YOUR VOICE

YOU ARE,

MY LOVE...

YOU ARE...

LIKE AN UNREAD CHAPTER OF A BOOK
I NEVER WANT TO CLOSE

THE MOST BEAUTIFUL PICTURE I'VE EVER SEEN
EVEN THOUGH YOU NEVER STOPPED TO POSE

YOU ARE
LIKE THE CLOUDS GENTLY FLOATING IN THE SKY
SIMPLY MESMERIZING AND ALWAYS CAPTURING MY EYE

THE MOST INTRIGUING SIGHT I'VE EVER SEEN
AND YOU DON'T EVEN TRY

YOU ARE
LOVE'S FREQUENCY
TRAVELING THROUGH SPACE AND TIME

THE MOST PERPLEXING YET EFFORTLESSLY EASY SOUL FOR ME TO
UNDERSTAND EVEN THOUGH YOU'RE NOT QUITE MINE,

YOU ARE
DARKNESS AND LIGHT , PEACE AND FIGHT, GROUNDED AND
FLIGHT,

EVERY FORM OF BEAUTY, COMPASSION, SENSUAL REACTIONS AND
THE CAUSE OF MY HIGHEST SATISFACTION
WHICH CAN ONLY BEGIN TO DESCRIBE ALL
THAT,

YOU ARE...

I WILL INTRODUCE YOU...

I know that you were
Waiting
For the real me to show up
But I was so afraid you wouldn't like her
So I chose to introduce you
To other stuff
Sarcasm, overt sexuality, and a series of Serious
Expectations...

You never got to see the beauty in me
That manifest in the form
Of patience, while waiting

You never got to experience my other world type passion
In the process of love making...

My kindness, comfort, and understanding

Instead, I was pretending
To be stronger than I am
Which came across as demanding

I should have introduced you to her
You would have loved her
Just as much as she loves you

I promise if I get a chance to get out the
Way,
I will introduce you...

The One...

I text in five-page letters
Never just
A sentence or two
Yet it would take
An encyclopedia of words to
Begin to Describe you
You are that tingling sensation
That moves up my right thigh
To the small of my back
You are the tear that falls from My left eye slowly
streaming across my left cheek
until it moisten my neck
You are the only one that takes my breath away, causing
an unbearable tightness in my chest
You are the essence of joy and optimist wonder
Your kisses are as electric as the sky
Dancing with thunder
I've spent hours upon hours wondering where you came
from
It's a question that may never
Have an answer
But I'm grateful you've come
Because you are,

The One...

CHAPTER 9 9:17

Truly Living...

Taking chances, with the hopes of achieving true Love, Success, and Joy when it appears you won't be the victor does not equate to irrational thinking,
It equates to,

Truly Living...

Don't undervalue those that love you immensely but don't know how to say it

By overvaluing those that don't love at all but know how to say it...

The purpose of our spirits descending to earth was to experience the experiences that can only be experienced with the senses made possible by the flesh.

Remember the flesh is temporary. Don't forget to experience the experiences that can only be experienced with the senses made possible by the flesh.

Because that is the purpose of our spirits descending to earth.

T.S. Davis

I will stop trying to find reasons to glorify people who are not really there for me...

Instead, I will magnify the way I show appreciation to those who are actually there for me.

T.S. Davis

When someone says your insecurities are pushing them away, push harder. I guarantee you once they leave so will the cause of your insecurities.

T.S. Davis

1221
Knowing the difference between living a life of desire and a life of purpose will help guide you toward a life of fulfillment and peace depending upon which one you choose.
T.S. Davis

MY 3...
YOU ARE MY JOY
MY ABSOLUTE REASON FOR BEING
THE MOMENT I SAW YOU
MY LIFE GAINED NEW MEANING
THE FIRST TIME I HEARD
YOUR HEARTBEAT
AND THE WARMTH OF YOUR CHEEKS
AGAINST MY CHEEKS
I COULD HARDLY SPEAK
I KNEW YOU WERE
THE VERY ESSENCE OF
WHAT MADE ME
ME
THEN GOD MULTIPLIED
THIS FEELING TIMES THREE
AND SHOWED ME WHAT
UNCONDITIONAL LOVE
SHOULD BE
HE ALLOWED ME TO
SEE
THAT REAL LOVE IS FREE
SELFLESS AND FORGIVING
THE MOMENT I MET YOU
I WANTED TO PROTECT YOU
AND START GIVING
ALL THAT I HAD
EVEN WHEN YOU ACT BAD
I'M STILL INCREDIBLY GLAD
THAT I'VE BEEN
ENTRUSTED WITH YOU
AMAZED THAT I WAS
ABLE TO PRODUCE
LIVES AS PHENOMENAL
AS MY TWO BOYS AND ONE GIRL
MY HEARTBEATS ,MY WHOLE WORLD
MY FOOTBALL, SOCCER AND DANCE TWIRL
MY TAPER, FADE AND LONG CURLS
SO DIFFERENT YET THE SAME
I LOVE YOU ALL MORE THAN YOU KNOW AND THAT WILL NEVER
CHANGE ♥

TO BE FREE...

EQUAL TO THE ABILITY TO DECIDE
WHAT THINGS MATTER MOST TO SELF
WITHOUT THE OBLIGATION OF FORCED
COMPLIANCE TO PLEASE SOMEONE ELSE

TO BE FREE
THE ABILITY TO GO TO THE HEIGHTS OF
WHICH YOU PLEASE
THE RIGHT TO EXPERIENCE FULL IMMERSIVE
WORSHIP ON YOUR FACE, HANDS, AND KNEES

NOT HAVING TO DO OR SAY
WHAT THE WORLD DEFINES AS ACCEPTED OR
OKAY

SIMPLY BEING A SIMPLE BEING
WITH THE CAPACITY
TO SHATTER THE WORLD'S PERCEPTIONS OF
THEIR PERFECT REALITY

IS TO ME
JUST A FEW EXAMPLES OF WHAT IT MEANS,

To be free...

CHAPTER 10 11:11

DAILY...

BEFORE YOU, I THOUGHT ABOUT LOVE AND THE
COMPLEXITIES OF LIFE
CONTINUOUSLY AND WITHOUT CEASING

YET IT WASN'T UNTIL YOU WALKED
ONTO MY PURPOSE PATH
DID I TRULY BEGIN TO COMPREHEND THERE MEANING

I KNEW I HAD A PASSION AND GIFT FOR
WRITING, YET YOU TAUGHT ME THE REASON

THOUGH YOUR EMOTIONS CHANGE AS FREQUENTLY AS
THE SEASON

YOU SIMPLY BEING YOU
HAS LED TO MY HEALING

THE RHYTHMIC VIBRATIONS
IN THE SUBTLE TONES OF YOUR VOICE SOMEHOW DICTATE
THE VARIOUS FLUCTUATIONS OF MY FEELINGS

I CAN EXPERIENCE SADNESS, HAPPINESS, LONELINESS AND
WHOLENESS WITHIN THE SPAN OF ONE OF OUR
CONVERSATIONS

SEE YOU ARE THE ONE FOR WHOM I'VE BEEN WAITING
I WILL WAIT ON YOU FOREVER IF I MUST
FOR I KNOW THAT A PART OF MY DESTINY
IS FOR YOU AND I TO BECOME
US
FALLING MORE IN LOVE,
DAILY...

MY FIRST REACTION...
YOUR EYES DRAW IN MY SOUL
I KNOW
YOU'RE FULL OF STORIES WAITING TO BE TOLD
YOUR EYES FEEL ME WITH JOY AND SENSATIONS
THAT NO WORDS HAVE BEEN INVENTED TO DESCRIBE
YOUR TOUCH MAKES ME BREATHE DEEPLY AND
FEEL FREELY
WHILE EXPERIENCING TINGLES, SHIVERS, AND
EMOTIONS
I DIDN'T NO I HAD IN ME
YOU MAKE ME FEEL COMPLETELY COMPLETE
MY HEART FORGETS
TO BEAT
WHENEVER YOU SPEAK
YOU'RE MY DREAM
RATHER I'M AWAKE OR ASLEEP
YOU ARE LOVE AND LIFE AT IT'S
PEAK
YOU GIVE ME STRENGTH
WHEN I FEEL WEAK
YOU ARE THE CULMINATION
OF EVERYTHING I'VE SOUGHT
AND EVERYTHING THAT I SEEK

YOU ARE YOU
YOU ARE EVERYTHING THIS IS IMPERFECT
PERFECTION

I WOULD BE INSANE
IF FALLING IN LOVE WITH YOU WAS NOT
MY FIRST REACTION...

YOU HAD POWER OVER MY HAPPINESS

MORE POWER THAN ANY ONE PERSON SHOULD
HAVE

I AM RULED BY MY EMOTIONS AND INTUITION

WHEN YOU BECAME MY EMOTIONS MY
INTUITION FOLLOWED

ALL I FELT WAS YOU
YOUR SADNESS, YOUR HAPPINESS, YOUR PAIN
AND YOUR JOY

I LOST ME WHEN I FOUND YOU
IT COULD HAVE BEEN SOMETHING AMAZING IF
ONLY YOU HAD LOVED ME THE WAY THAT I
LOVED YOU

BECAUSE THEN I COULD HAVE LOVED ME
TOO...
AND THAT UNFORTUNATELY
IS,

THE SAD TRUTH...

I SEE YOU...

YOUR EYES DRAW ME IN

IT'S LIKE YOUR SMILE IS A POET
AND YOUR LAUGHTER IS A PEN
WRITING POETRY IN MY SOUL
OVER AND OVER AGAIN

YOU GLOW WITH HAPPINESS
YOUR SPIRIT EXUDES SILENT YET BLARING SIGNS
THAT YOU ARE COMPLETELY DIFFERENT FROM THE REST

YOU ARE UNIQUE,YOU ARE SPECIAL, YOU ARE MY TEST THAT I
MUST PASS

WILL I CONTINUE TO LIVE IN THE PAST?

OR EMBRACE MY FUTURE, GOING AGAINST THE ROUTINE OF
WHAT I WOULD USUALLY DO?

A HOPEFUL ROMANTIC, MOST OF THE TIME VERY NOSTALGIC

REMINISCING ON OLD MOMENTS THAT MY JOY HAS BEEN
CONNECTED TO

DAYDREAMING, CONSTANTLY MISSING OPPORTUNITIES TO
DO EVERYTHING THAT I'M SUPPOSED TO DO

NOT THIS TIME...
NO THIS TIME I WON'T MISS MY BLESSING
BECAUSE I RECOGNIZE THAT YOU ARE MY JOY IN THE
PRESENT
AND,

I SEE YOU...

FOREVER MY MUSE...

YOUR POSITIVITY ALWAYS GETS TO ME
YOU SPEAK WITH THE HEART OF A POET

YOUR INTELLECT IS UNMATCHED
YOU ARE THE WISE BEYOND YOUR YEARS I JUST
WONDER IF YOU KNOW IT

YOUR OPTIMISM IS ASTOUNDING
YOU ARE THE CAUSE OF MY SMILES AND MY HAPPY
TEARS

YOUR STRENGTH CONSTANTLY STRENGTHENS ME
YOU ARE THE CURE TO MY FEARS

YOUR CREATIVITY INSPIRES ME
YOU ARE THE REASON MY HEART SPEAKS POETRY IT
HASN'T SPOKEN IN YEARS

YOUR LOVE IS SOMETHING I PRAY I NEVER LOSE
YOU ARE MY HEART, MY SOUL,AND

FOREVER MY MUSE...

DON'T LET HIM TAKE ME…

HE IS SAYING EVERYTHING I WANTED YOU TO
SAY
HE TEXT ME EVERY NIGHT,AND AT THE DAWN
OF EACH NEW DAY
HE MAKES ME LAUGH,GIGGLE AND SMILE
WITHOUT CEASING
HE LISTENS WHEN I VENT AND RESPONDS TO
ME QUICKLY,
LATELY I'VE BEEN PICTURING WHAT IT WILL
FEEL LIKE FOR HIM TO KISS ME
HE IS DOING EVERYTHING CORRECTLY
ACCEPT BE YOU
OF COURSE THAT IS SOMETHING ONLY YOU
CAN DO
HOWEVER, BEING HIMSELF MAY BE ALL THAT I
NEED
SO IF YOU LOVE ME, I MEAN REALLY LOVE ME
SAY SOMETHING, DO SOMETHING NOW
AND,

DON'T LET HIM TAKE ME…

NOW...

ACCEPTING THAT IT DOESN'T HAVE TO BE YOU
IS SOMETHING THAT I ALREADY KNEW
BUT SIMPLY DID NOT WANT TO DO

IT'S FUNNY HOW WE GROW
IN SPITE OF HOW MUCH WE RESIST

IT'S STRANGE HOW YOU WERE NEVER TRULY HERE
YET YOU ARE THE ONE THAT I MISS

MAYBE ITS
BECAUSE I FEEL LIKE I FELL
BUT I MISSED YOU OR YOU MISSED ME

ONLY TIME WILL TELL
ALL OF THE SIGNALS WE DIDN'T HEAR
AND THE SIGNS WE DIDN'T SEE

THOSE THINGS THAT WERE RIGHT THERE IN FRONT
OF US
YET WE LOOKED RIGHT PASS

THE OPPORTUNITIES OF HAPPINESS THAT WE SHOULD
HAVE CHERISHED
INSTEAD WE CARELESSLY TOSSED INTO THE
LIFE'S TRASH

THOUGH MY ONLY GOAL WAS TO LOVE YOU
SOMEWAY SOME HOW
I HAVE TO ADMIT DEFEAT AND SIMPLY
ACCEPT THAT YOU DON'T WANT MY LOVE
RIGHT,
NOW...

EVERYONE ELSE...

IF YOU CAN'T SEE YOUR GREATNESS
HOW CAN ANYONE ELSE?

WHY SHOULD THEY APPRECIATE YOU
IF YOU DON'T APPRECIATE YOURSELF?

STOP PRAYING TO BE RICH
UNTIL YOU UNDERSTAND WEALTH

WHY COMPLAIN ABOUT BEING SICK
LIKE YOU'RE NOT RESPONSIBLE FOR YOUR
HEALTH

STOP PUSHING PEOPLE AWAY, THEN
WONDER WHY YOU'RE ALWAYS
BY YOURSELF.

YOU'RE REAPING WHAT YOU'VE SOWN
SO PLEASE STOP BLAMING,

EVERYONE ELSE...

QUITE THE SILENCE...

Why does silence echo the loudest when I'm alone

Reminding me of just how deafening the screams of loneliness are

Why does each tear
Feel just a tad bit heavier than the last
Streaming down my cheeks tearing away at my happiness mask

My "I'm feeling much better today" mask...
My "of course I feel like laughing at your jokes" mask...
My "yes I'm good, I've got everything under control"
Mask...

Each tear loaded with unfiltered honesty
Revealing my vulnerability

Completely exposing me
My fragility
That I try to pretend does not exist

Alone in silence
But not really
Yet definitely alone
But the silence has a deep penetrating tone of despair

Reminding me of those I love even though I know
They don't care

Reminding that yes I'm smart, beautiful and rare
Yet still not enough

Yes I'm incredibly strong
Yet still not tough
Reminding me that

I know

Why silence echoes the loudest when I'm alone

It's Because I am alone and there is no one here with me to help,
Quite the silence...

LIFE
How many of
You observe
The beauty of trees
In case you go
Blind
Or enjoy
Standing upright
In case you lose
The functionality of your spine
Actively engaged in learning
And processing
In case you lose the
Abilities of your mind
Or stand perfectly still
Just to feel the
Movement of time
See most of you are living but haven't quite
Lived
Most of you have given
But don't appreciate
The ability to give
All you do is do
Without any reason
You see the weather change but
Don't appreciate the season
You ask about the purpose of life
But care not about the meaning.
No comprehension
Of my reasoning
for which
I hope you are gleaning
The need for you to
Be keenly aware
And grateful for being
A being
Capable of feeling
And perceiving
This Perspective
Of life
So that one day You will realize
That knowing the beauty
Of being alive
Is the greatest insight…

Stained Sheets...
We're so accustomed
To being told to look for the
Purity in white sheets
We're told to overlook the blood stains
And the pain that came from them
I wonder if we caused the bloodshed
Or continuously ridiculed the ones who bled
Who would have their rights to be mad
Washed away
Who would be told to be silent and just pray
And be grateful for living in better days
Ignore the K, the K, the Ks in our community use kill
Our men and lock them away
How did they get there
We didn't bring them in
We don't import or export
Liquor, crack cocaine or heroin
We don't pollute the water
Causing our kids to drink poison
But we should be tired of watching it happen
Yeah I wrote this, but I'm tired of rapping
I'm tired of listening to good speeches and clapping
Tired of being told
We only belong
On one spot on the map and
I'm tired of hoping that the things
We need will hopefully
Begin manifesting
I'm tired of seeing young black men die unjustly and then reacting
I'm tired...
It's time to make what needs to happen
Happen
Time to stop clapping
And start clapping back
Time to make the predator the prey
And develop a plan of attack
Time to rein in our dominion and take our world back
Time to give back the word black
In exchange for supreme
Acknowledgement of our royal blood
And our connection to the Heavenly King!
Time to live our true reality and give them back their American Dream.

Purpose is not a popularity contest.

It is about passion and pursuit. It is about fulfilling
your reason for being. The moment you make it
about anything else is the moment that you lose
focus. When you lose focus you lose clarity without
clarity, you lose sight of your vision. Without vision, it
is impossible to see where you are going. If you
cannot see where you are going it is impossible to get
there!

Made in the USA
Monee, IL
05 May 2020